ANIMALS GROWING UP™

HOW BEARS GROW UP

Enslow Publishing
101 W. 23rd Street
Suite 240
New York, NY 10011
USA
enslow.com

Heather Moore Niver

WORDS TO KNOW

cub A baby bear.

den A place where wild animals live.

hibernate To spend the winter sleeping or resting.

mammal An animal that has a backbone and hair; females usually give birth to live babies and produce milk to feed their young.

nurse To feed a baby milk produced from the body.

predator An animal that kills and eats other animals to survive.

sibling A brother or sister.

sow An adult female mammal, such as a bear.

species A group of living things that are alike and have the same scientific name.

CONTENTS

BABY BEARS

Bear cubs look cute and fuzzy. They tumble and play together. It looks like a whole lot of fun! But there is more than fun happening. They are practicing for life in the wild!

FAST FACT

There are eight **species**, or kinds, of bear in the world.

Brown bear cubs wrestle in the forest.

FIRST BORN

When bear cubs are born, they are helpless. They cannot see. They cannot hear. They do not have any teeth! They have very little to no fur.

A 10-day-old black bear cub sleeps.

FAST FACT

Baby bear cubs weigh less than one pound (454 grams) when they are born.

MAMMAL BABIES

Bears are mammals. Mammals feed their babies milk. Mother bears nurse their cubs. Mother bears carry their cubs by their heads!

A panda nurses her cub.

HIBERNATION

Bears that live in cold areas rest all winter, or hibernate. Their cubs are born in a den in the winter or early spring. They stay in the den until spring.

FAST FACT

A sow may have between one and three cubs at a time.

A brown bear cub comes out of the den.

SPRING

When the weather warms up in the spring, hibernating bears leave the den. It is time to find food! The cubs follow their mother. She shows them how to hunt.

FAST FACT

Sloth bear mothers carry their babies on their backs while they hunt.

A sloth bear carries a cub on her back while the other cub follows her.

DINNER!

Bears eat both plants and animals. Bears look for ripe food, such as fruit, roots, and nuts. They have great senses of smell, sight, and hearing.

A brown bear cub munches on some oats.

PLAYTIME

The cubs play and wrestle. They are learning to fight and defend themselves. Cubs also need to learn how to climb trees to escape danger.

FAST FACT

If bear cubs play too rough, their mother will gently whack them with her paw.

A black bear cub climbs onto a branch to look out.

17

BROTHERS AND SISTERS

Bear cubs usually grow up with their mothers. They leave when they are almost two years old. Brothers and sisters might stay together for another year. Siblings help protect each other.

Two brown bear cubs walk together and keep each other safe.

FAST FACT

A baby bear can survive on its own once it stops nursing.

CAREFUL CUBS

Adult bears do not have any predators. But cubs and smaller sows have to be careful. Large male bears or older bears could attack them. Mothers sometimes attack to protect their cubs.

FAST FACT

Humans are a bear's main predator. They will hunt big or small bears.

A polar bear protects her cubs from danger.

21

ALL GROWN UP

A grizzly bear cub is considered an adult when it is five years old. This is when the females are old enough to have cubs of their own.

A grizzly bear leads her young cubs into the world.

23

LEARN MORE

Books

Boothroyd, Jennifer. *From Cub to Panda*. Minneapolis, MN: Lerner Publications, 2017.

Gunderson, Megan M. *Bears Eat and Grow*. Minneapolis, MN: Magic Wagon, 2015.

Kelley, K. C. *Baby Bears*. Mankato, MN: Amicus, 2018.

Websites

National Geographic Kids: Brown Bear
kids.nationalgeographic.com/animals/brown-bear/#brown-bear-fish-stream.jpg
Learn all about brown bears, also known as grizzly bears.

San Diego Zoo Kids: Polar Bear
kids.sandiegozoo.org/animals/polar-bear
Read about polar bears and watch videos.

INDEX

Published in 2019 by Enslow Publishing, LLC.
101 W. 23rd Street, Suite 240, New York, NY 10011

Copyright © 2019 by Enslow Publishing, LLC.
All rights reserved.

No part of this book may be reproduced by any means without the written permission of the publisher.

Library of Congress Cataloging-in-Publication Data
Names: Niver, Heather Moore, author.
Title: How bears grow up / Heather Moore Niver.
Description: New York, NY : Enslow Publishing, 2019. | Series: Animals growing up | Includes bibliographical references and index. | Audience: Grades K to 3.
Identifiers: LCCN 2017044741 | ISBN 9780766096356 (library bound) | ISBN 9780766096363 (pbk.) | ISBN 9780766096370 (6 pack)
Subjects: LCSH: Bears—Development—Juvenile literature. | Bear cubs—Juvenile literature.
Classification: LCC QL737.C27 N58 2017 | DDC 599.7813/92—dc23
LC record available at https://lccn.loc.gov/2017044741

Printed in the United States of America

To Our Readers: We have done our best to make sure all website addresses in this book were active and appropriate when we went to press. However, the author and the publisher have no control over and assume no liability for the material available on those websites or on any websites they may link to. Any comments or suggestions can be sent by email to customerservice@enslow.com.

Photo Credits: Cover, p. 1 Thomas Kokta/Photographer's Choice RF/Getty Images; pp. 4-23 (background image) Volodymyr Burdiak/Shutterstock.com; p. 5 Erik Mandre/Shutterstock.com; p. 7 Suzi Eszterhas/Minden Pictures/Getty Images; p. 9 Keren Su/Corbis Documentary/Getty Images; p. 11 © iStockphoto.com/bas0r; p. 13 Sylvain Cordier/Science Source; p. 15 Staffan Widstrand/Corbis Documentary /Getty Images; p. 17 Holly Kuchera/Shutterstock.com; p. 19 Gudkov Andrey /Shutterstock.com; p. 21 USO/iStock/Thinkstock; p. 23 Hainstock Photography /Shutterstock.com.